Living Virtuously

A 31-Day Devotional to Inspire Wellness for the Mind, Body & Spirit

Nichole M. Thomas, INHC

Living Virtuously
©2017 by Nichole Thomas

This book is also available as an ebook.
Visit www.VirtuousLiving.com

Requests for information should be addressed to:

Good Success Publishing
P.O. Box 5072
Upper Marlboro, MD 20775

ISBN 8 978-0-9981597-0-6

Library of Congress Control Number: 2017900040
This book is printed on acid-free paper

All scripture quotations, unless otherwise indicated, are taken from the New King James Version. Used by permission. All rights reserved.

The book uses standard cooking measurements and times. However due to the skill, tools and technique differences in people, cooking times may very.

The Author and Publishers of this book are not responsible for any adverse reactions to the recipes or activities herein. Additionally, the statements in this book have not been evaluated by the U.S. Food and Drug Administration. This book is not meant to treat, diagnose, cure or prevent any sickness or disease.

For the aforementioned reasons, to the fullest extent of the law, the Author and Publishers do not accept any legal duty of care, liability or responsibility for the effectiveness or accuracy of this book. "Recommendations" or any other terms to that effect disclaim any liability, loss, damage or risk that may be claimed-directly-or indirectly- of the use and or application of the contents of this book.

Cover/Interior graphic design: Titus V. Thomas
Photography: Davide De Pas and Karla Ticas
Style Team: Endia Leonard, Jada Jenkins, Jodie Johnson, Lola Okanlawon
Printed in the United States of America

Contents

"Do something better today, than you did yesterday. That's Virtuous Living"

-Nichole Thomas

Acknowledgements

To the love of my life, Etan

Thank you for loving me back to life, and for helping me continue to grow into the woman of God you always saw me as. I honor you for your faith, your strength, your vision and leadership for our family. You are a wonderful Husband and Father, and I respect the man of God that you are. Your love and care in times when my health and faith have been challenged are one of the reasons this book means so much.

For Malcolm, Imani & Sierra

You are the greatest joys of my life. I am so blessed to be your Mom, and I am so thankful that we are all learning the importance of nourishing our temples together. I pray that you will always know my reason for fussing with you, removing foods, reintroducing foods, creating new products, and even forcing schools to do right by your health is because I LOVE YOU! I see the amazing things that God has placed inside of each of you, and want God to get the glory from your lives! I couldn't be more proud of you, and I can't wait to see what life holds for you. You can do all things through Christ who strengthens you. I have your back, always

For Mom, Dad, & Carlton

Mi Familia - I love you guys to the ends of the Earth. Mom, words can't express how much you mean to me. The way you constantly show me what a Virtuous Woman looks like, and how you love me! Thank you for being my North Star. Dad and Carlton, thank you for all the love and support you have always given me. Everything we have been through has and will always be for our development and for God's glory. I am thankful that God knew exactly what family I need to be a part of, and I am more thankful now than ever before. I love you!

To Pastor John and First Lady Trina Jenkins, my spiritual Mom & Dad

Thank you for you love, support, mentorship and guidance over the years. You have consistently shown Etan & I what being a family of faith looks like. I don't know if you will ever truly know how much you mean to me, but I give God glory for you both.

For Julie & Bronique

The sisters I never knew I needed, but always had. Thank you for being the fire that pushes me to answer God's call.

To my E-13 sisters

Amos 9, and I love you with all my heart. To all the phenomenal women who have prayed for me, encouraged, uplifted, blessed, texted, tweeted, called, hugged, baby-sat or simply-believed that this would one day happen, thank you.

To God be the Glory!

Foreword

Beloved, I pray that you may prosper in all things and be in health, just as you soul prospers. *2 John 1:2*

These words were written by John centuries ago. And they are echoed today in Living Virtuously by Nichole Thomas. She presents life-changing information in a manner that is clear, comprehensive, and easy to understand. She provides an integrative path to address the most important aspects of life: Spiritual Health, Emotional Health, Physical Health, and Self-Love. She artfully combines the Word of God, her expertise in Integrative Nutrition, and her personal experiences to create daily readings and exercises that are sure to motivate and inspire. Then, she walks you through the process of incorporating these principles into your life in a manner that benefits both those experienced in health and nutrition and the novice alike.

One of the most powerful activities in this book is what Nichole calls "Nighttime Reflection". Here, she challenges you to look back over the day and acknowledge your accomplishments as well as those things for which you are most grateful. Then, she empowers you by asking you to affirm the following: "Since I can do ALL things through Christ, tomorrow I will: _____". You fill in the blank.

What an impactful way to end each day! Nichole has shared simple but effective principles with my husband, Pastor Jenkins and me that have helped us make wise decisions to improve our health. It is her love for God and people that led her to write this book. If living a victorious life is something that you desire to accomplish, then this is the book for you. I encourage you to grab your Bible, a pen, and your journal. Find a quiet place and allow Nichole Thomas to guide you towards reaching that goal as you work through Living Virtuously.

First Lady Trina Jenkins
First Baptist Church of Glenarden

"Love God,
love yourself,
love people."

-Nichole Thomas

Introduction

I am ALIVE today because God kept me! It really is that simple. There were many times in my journey to healing where I almost didn't make it, but God said not so! As a girl, I dealt with chronic stomach pain, eczema, attention deficitdisorder (ADD), hyperactivity and a bunch of other challenges. Fast forward to my adult life just before I became pregnant with my second child and all hell broke loose. Simply stated, I was so sick that seeing my 30th birthday seemed like wishful thinking. Constant, indescribable pain, memory loss, weight gain, thyroid conditions and misdiagnosis after misdiagnosis left me depressed, angry and flat out exhausted. The good thing about serving a God who knows all and sees all is that even the things doctors can sometimes miss, He Can Heal!

That's when God used my tragedy and turned it into triumph, and Virtuous Living was born. After being diagnosed with Celiac disease, and finally coming to understand how severe food allergies were the cause of my poor health, I learned that the right foods had the ability to heal me. That the word of God is true, and "what the devil meant for evil, God continues to use it for good." In my case it wasn't just for my good, but for the world's good. Virtuous Living's products and services are impacting the World through health, wellness and most importantly renewed, power-filled relationships with Christ.

I can't tell you how thrilled I am that you're reading this book. My heart's desire is to help you see the transformation you want in your own lives come to pass, through Christ! The Bible teaches us in Philippians 4:13 that we 'can do all things through Christ who strengthens" us! You have to first believe the Word is true. Not just a book to be read when you need comfort, but the sword with which you fight daily. You must know that God's desire for you is that you are healthy, wealthy and wise. Knowing and fully understanding this means that you must use all the tools in your arsenal to fight this battle. And though it's a battle, I have good news ...YOU WIN! The battle is indeed fixed, and all you need to do is show up. Show up daily in your life, ready to be led by the Holy Spirit to take back what I believe is every believer's birthright in Christ: optimal health and extraordinary wellness.

This book is designed to walk you through 31 days of transformation. I created it so that it divides each day into 3 categories with room for you to journal your thoughts, prayers, meditations and triumphs. Each day begins with a devotion and a scripture. This is for your **Spiritual Health**, and in this section there is room for you to meditate on and write down all that the that the Holy Spirit guides you to think and pray on. Next is the **Emotional Health** section. This step is very important because we often sabotage our life because of emotional challenges. God gave us an entire range of emotions, and most of us only utilize a few of them. Emotional health can be one of the hardest things to work on, but without it, we will never truly be well. So please pay extra attention to what comes up for you.

The final section focuses on your **Physical Health** and the function of this section is to assist you in making nutrient rich, healthy food choices that meet the demands of your lifestyle. It is also to introduce you to new methods designed to bring a sense of balance into your life. Whether that is a new yoga pose for more restorative sleep, deep breathing techniques for a clearer mind, or fiber rich food choices that help with the elimination of toxins and negative emotions. This section is for your overall physical well being. Each devotion is designed to be 2 days in length, allowing you time to focus, pray and feel the changes as they take place. There is also a nightly check-in to encourage more restful sleep. I hope that you are as excited as I am for you to start this book. I pray that with your desire to start comes a commitment to devote yourself to growing in the areas in which you need change. Does weight loss, stronger muscles, better relationships, wiser food choices, financial health, free flowing creativity, sleeping more soundly, more joy, a fulfilling career, and a strong relationship with the Lord sound good to you? All of this and so much more is what God has in store for you. I praise God for what is about to take place in your life!

Confessions of Faith

Proverbs 3:5 & 6 says, "Trust in the Lord with all your heart, and lean not to your own understanding, but in all your ways acknowledge Him, and He will direct your path." This is where the good part starts. If you don't know Christ, He can't direct or guide you. Knowing Jesus for yourself is what makes this book come alive. It's not a gimmick or a scheme. It's not magic and God isn't a genie. Having a real relationship with Jesus Christ is what will ignite you and help you walk in divine wellness. *(Shout out to my Sister, Dr. Celeste Owens). Do you know Christ as your Lord and Savior? Do you believe he is the Son of God? Do you believe he died and rose for your sins? Do you desire to have Him as Lord of your life? If the answer to these questions is yes, then let's do it.

Repeat after me:

Dear Jesus,

I repent of my sins, and I ask you to come into my heart. Be the Lord of my life, heal me, restore me, and equip me to be all that you have for me to be. I receive you as Lord, and I thank you for loving me. Amen! If you prayed that prayer and believed in your heart that Jesus Christ is Lord of your life, the Bible says, you are saved! To God be all the glory.

Please write your name and the date of your commitment to complete
this book here:

_____

Now all you need to do is to find a bible teaching church, and connect with a ministry that can continue to help you grow in the things of God. For a list of resources in your area visit **www.virtuousliving.com**

Medical Disclaimer

This book is not meant to treat or diagnose any disease, illness or conditions. I am not a Physician and the opinions and perspectives in this book are based on my own experiences. As a trained and Board Certified Integrative Health Coach, my expertise is in the area of nutritional education and lifestyle modification for optimum health. My view is a holistic one, that includes my Christian faith. Please take great care that you are feeling well and healthy during the next 31 days. Be wise in making changes or introducing new foods or activities, so that you can enjoy the outcomes of this work.

At any time during the course of this book should you begin to feel badly, please contact your Physician immediately.

Now as my mom would say, "Go forth for Jesus!"

14

Day 1 & 2

Spiritual Health: 1 Peter 3:3-4 (NKJV) What kind of wife are you?

3 *"Do not let your adornment be merely outward arranging the hair, wearing gold, or putting on fine apparel* **4** *rather let it be the hidden person of the heart, with the incorruptible beauty of a gentle and quiet spirit, which is very precious in the sight of God."*

My church home is THE First Baptist Church of Glenarden in Maryland. My husband and I are blessed to have a close relationship with our Pastor and First Lady. While my husband and I were engaged, my First Lady, Mrs. Trina told me that the way to a man's heart wasn't only through his stomach, but through his ears. I laughed, but now, 13 years of marriage and 3 kids later I know she was right.

As a wife, I am often privy to insights from the Holy Spirit that my husband hasn't been shown. Just to clarify, this is NOT because I am more spiritual than he. This is a function of my role in our marriage. He provides, protects, covers and will do battle with any enemy that comes our way. His job is not, however, to be surveyor of the land, or to be on the wall constantly praying before such attacks happen. That's my job. With that knowledge can sometimes come a self-exalting spirit. But if we are to be the help-meet God desires for us to be, we must understand that we are not our husbands' teachers. We are to assist them by bringing helpful conversation and perspective to situations concerning our relationships and our lives.

Now don't get thrown off if you're not married. The simple truth is that even in our single-hood we are committed to Christ. Marriage to Christ can be just as hard as marriage to another human being, even harder if we are honest. We are to honor Him in all that we do, consult with him on what's best for our lives, be in a posture of submission to the Lord regardless of the circumstance and we can't even have an argument about it! Well, I guess you could, but you might feel a bit silly fussing at the ceiling. (I've done it many times.) The Word goes on to say in 1 Peter 3:5-6, "For this is the way the holy women of the past who put their hope in God used to adorn themselves. They submitted themselves to their own husbands, like Sarah, who obeyed Abraham and called him her lord. You are her daughters if you do what is right and do not give way to fear."

The end of verse 6 is what really gets me about this passage: "if we do what is right and do not give way to fear." Fear is what I sometimes struggled with. Fear of not being heard, of losing my voice, or that I didn't agree with my husband's perspective. But in order to be the kind of 'wife' we need to be we must not give way to fear. This is what enables us to stand, with gentleness and peacefulness because we are totally and completely submitted to the Lordship of Jesus in our lives. With prayer and a whole lot of practice, I'm finally learning how to bless my husband with my tone as well as my words. Our desire should be to glorify God with a sweet and gentle spirit. Not as a pushover, but standing in the full integrity of who God has called us to be, and understanding the power of prayer, a tender touch and a gentle word.

Emotional Health:

1. How can you work on reflecting a more gentle manner in your marriage or relationships?
_____
_____

2. What are some examples of gentle responses you can give? _____
_____

3. Do you think this will enhance your relationship? In what way?_____
_____
_____

4. How have confrontational responses or being argumentative caused harm to your relationships? _____
_____
_____

5. How does this (submissive posture) actually release you from stress and fear? _____
_____
_____
_____
_____
_____
_____
_____
_____
_____
_____

Physical Health:

As you focus on operating in gentleness, meditate on today's scripture. Avoid red meat, as foods have energy. Red meat typically has a more aggressive energy and will not aid you in accomplishing your goal of meekness.

Consider yoga or a slower, longer walk for exercise for the next 2 days. Also think about using lavender in your home or workplace to bring a sense of calm and peace.

Self Love Checklist:

Show love to yourself with these daily exercises

- Long, gentle walk, swimming or yoga
- Added Organic veggies to meal
- Drink H2O
- Talk with friends
- Deep Breathing
- Essential Oils for relaxation
- Herbal Tea
- Oil Pulling
- Spend time in nature
- Laughing
- Dancing
- Prayer

Nighttime reflection:

Today I accomplished:_____

Since I can do ALL things through Christ, tomorrow I will:

_____

_____

_____

I'm grateful for?_____

Journal your thoughts/prayers:

_____

_____

_____

_____

_____

_____

_____

_____

_____

_____

_____

_____

_____

_____

_____

_____

_____

_____

_____

_____

Days 3 & 4

Spiritual Health: Isaiah 55 (NKJV) Won't He Do It?

Abundance. Most of us have a hard time getting our minds around the term. It creates feelings of confusion, and challenges our feelings of modesty even if that is also incorrect thinking. It forces us to look introspectively at what we truly feel we deserve. All of this can be uncomfort-able, and well, we just choose to stay stuck in the attitude of lack to which we've grown accus-tomed. I want to show you today that this thinking is not only false, but in direct contradiction to who God is, and what he has for you.

Isaiah 55 shows us that God's abundance is for us. Not only in the areas of spiritual wealth and relationship, but in all possible aspects of our lives. The Bible says that God's ways are higher than our ways, and His thoughts higher than our thoughts. His Word shows us his Ways. Coming into alignment in our thinking allows room for God's Word to bring abundance into our lives. Our affirming response to God's Word gives place for expansion.

And expansion is simply shifting expectation from lack to greater. Believe in faith that you have ALL that you require to be obedient to the voice of the Lord. This is very different from having all you need. Believe that you and your family are operating in divine health, wealth and wellness and that you are functioning efficiently and effectively.

Knowing that your heavenly Father has all that you need in His hands, and that He desires to bless you!

Emotional Health:

1. What does the concept of abundance bring up for you? Do you feel that it's for everyone else but you?

_____

_____

_____

2. Does abundance feel wrong to you as a Christian? Why or why not? _____

_____

_____

_____

3. How will focusing on God's abundance change your daily thoughts?

_____

_____

_____

_____

_____

_____

_____

_____

_____

_____

_____

_____

_____

_____

_____

_____

_____

_____

_____

Physical Health:

The next two days will be about activating your faith in the area of abundance. Try to engage in physical activities that you have not tried before. Look for someone and share what you are doing with them, maybe your spouse or a close friend. Try a new workout, expecting God to give you more than enough strength to get through it. Maybe you try a new Zumba class, or try out a new instructor at your favorite gym.

Be wise though. Do NOT decide to do something that requires a new level of preparation like walk for 39 miles, start Cross-fit elite, or climb a mountain. All things will come with time, but if one of those things is your goal, ask God for the right trainer that can get you on track to train better and safer.

Dietary abundance: Say a different prayer at every meal for the next two days. Think of words that are synonymous with abundance, like plenty, lavish, ample, bounty. Make your meals with ample amounts of fresh fruits and vegetables and choose a splurge. Not something sweet or a junk food (fast food), but something like grass-fed, organic meats, or wild caught seafood. Eat well during the next two days, knowing that God is able to make this and all other goodness abound in your life.

Self Love Checklist:

Show love to yourself with these daily exercises

- Long, gentle walk, swimming or yoga
- Added Organic veggies to meal
- Drink H2O
- Talk with friends
- Deep Breathing
- Essential Oils for relaxation
- Herbal Tea
- Oil Pulling
- Spend time in nature
- Laughing
- Dancing
- Prayer

Nighttime reflection:

Today I accomplished:_____

Since I can do ALL things through Christ, tomorrow I will:

_____

_____

_____

I'm grateful for?_____

Journal your thoughts/prayers:

_____

_____

_____

_____

_____

_____

_____

_____

_____

_____

_____

_____

_____

_____

_____

_____

_____

_____

_____

_____

Days 5 & 6

Spiritual Health: Acts 5:38-39 (NKJV) The Purpose of Purpose

38 *"And now I say to you, keep away from these men and let them alone; for if this plan or this work is of men, it will come to nothing;* **39** *but if it is of God, you cannot overthrow it lest you even be found to fight against God."*

When my husband and I got married, we had just entered his 4th season in the NBA. We had been together since our freshman year in college, and neither of us were raised extraordinarily wealthy. My husband however is a brilliant business man, and has used great wisdom when dealing with our finances. After we got married we realized we were in a position where we didn't have any needs...or wants. Everything was great, but why then was I so miserable? I'm sure you're thinking, "Seriously? What could you have had to complain about?"

You're right, on paper I didn't have anything to complain about, I had a great life, was married to the man of my dreams, but my heart was still unfulfilled. Why? The answer is because I wasn't clear on what my purpose was, and what season I had just entered into. The seasons of our lives can often alter the appearance of our purpose, but the purpose itself never changes. I soon learned after we had lost our 3rd family member, one of which was a matriarch of our family, that my purpose was to be in intercession for my husband, to diligently protect my marriage in prayer, and to be sensitive to the Holy Spirit and the atmosphere inside my home.

Now looking back, that purpose has changed only slightly. I am still to pray diligently for my husband, marriage, and children, and to foster a loving, peaceful environment in my home, but I am also to share the love of Jesus through health, wellness, food and faith. I'm grateful to be growing in so many areas, and have had a ton of challenges with staying focused. I already told you about the ADD thing!! But God always brings me back with the question "What did I call YOU to?"

Doing what someone else is called to robbed me of joy, it stole my confidence, and destroyed my peace. I even lost the ability to enjoy the life I was blessed to have because I was always comparing someone else's life to mine. When you walk in the purpose that God has for you no one can stand against you, or they will soon realize they are fighting against God himself. Your life isn't meant for anyone else, so "do you!" Seek the Lord on what your purpose is, and once you get the vision, hold on to it for dear life.

For the next two days, spend time in prayer about your purpose. Read Acts chapter 5, and write your thoughts below. God has a very specific plan for you and your gift is not like anyone else's. We need you; the World needs your gift so that God can be glorified in all areas.

Emotional Health:

1. Do you know what God has called you to do?_____

_____

_____

_____

2. Does your purpose scare you?_____

_____

_____

_____

3. Why or why not? _____

_____

_____

Journal your thoughts/prayers:

_____

_____

_____

_____

_____

_____

_____

_____

_____

_____

_____

_____

_____

_____

Physical Health:

The next two days will be about prayer and meditating on the Word. You might want to commit to slowing down on heavy foods that require a great deal of energy to digest properly. Try replacing a meal or two with juicing or green smoothies. Stay well-hydrated and eat lots of fresh fruits and vegetables. Listen for God's voice when deciding on what to eat and drink, as this will also aid in strengthening your ear for Him. Drink lots of water, tea with raw honey, and eat as many veggies as possible. Avoid meats unless necessary for lifestyle and dietary requirements due to medication. (If at any point during this time you start to not feel well, please consult your physician immediately.) Always listen to your body and nourish it well.

*This book is not meant to treat or diagnose any conditions. Please take great care that you are feeling well and healthy during the next 26 days. Be sure to use your Self Love Checklist and be extra gentle with yourself during your time of prayer and meditation.

Self Love Checklist:

Show love to yourself with these daily exercises

- Long, gentle walk, swimming or yoga
- Added Organic veggies to meal
- Drink H2O
- Talk with friends
- Deep Breathing
- Essential Oils for relaxation
- Herbal Tea
- Oil Pulling
- Spend time in nature
- Laughing
- Dancing
- Prayer

Nighttime reflection:

Today I accomplished:_____

Since I can do ALL things through Christ, tomorrow I will:

_____

_____

_____

_____

I'm grateful for?_____

Journal your thoughts/prayers:

_____

_____

_____

_____

_____

_____

_____

_____

_____

_____

_____

_____

_____

_____

_____

_____

_____

_____

_____

_____

_____

Juicing Recipes
Each recipe makes 64 ounces of juice.

Mrs. Green Jeans - This is simply to detoxify the system and bring back a slight increase of alkalinity. Also a great source of B vitamins

4 apples, cored
2-3 cucumbers
Handful of parsley
2 handfuls of spinach
2 stalks of kale
1 bunch of celery
1 lemon
1 tsp. fresh ginger

Guts & Glory - This juice is perfect to help with hydration and elimination, which can help to heal the gut, which studies show is the root of great health. High in Vitamin C it is also an immune booster.

10 pieces of beets (if packaged, make sure their organic)
1 bunch of celery
1 handful cilantro
1 tsp. fresh ginger
1 cucumber
2 lemons
10 romaine lettuce leaves
1 handful of spinach
15 carrots

Big Red - A support system for your adrenals, kidneys and liver, this beautiful crimson juice helps your body by reducing the amount of toxins in your blood. It is also acts as a toner for the nervous system.

6 apples, cored and seeded
10 pieces of beets (if packaged, make sure their organic)
1 bunch of celery
1 handful cilantro
1 cucumber
1 lemon
2 tomatoes
15 carrots

Days 7 & 8

Spiritual Health: Psalms 133:2-3 (NKJV) Run To Your Blessing

When I was 18, I was a student and Women's Basketball player at Syracuse University (SU). I left the comfortable climate of sunny Southern California for brutal snow-filled days in Syracuse, New York. It wasn't long after my arrival that I met a tall, smart, handsome kid from Tulsa, Oklahoma. We were introduced to one another by our respective coaches, and then again by friends. Everyone except us knew that we were meant to be. I look back now and laugh because who would have guessed that almost 20 years, and 3 kiddos later we would be happily married and walking out God's plan for our lives.

What you don't know about my story is WHY I left sunny California!!! As a girl I had a lot of gifts and talents, but I was heartbroken at 15yrs old over my parents' recent divorce. Involved in everything from youth ministry to show business, I had no time time for dating. Not long before my 17 birthday I began dating and my very first relationship ended in Rape. Yes, I know you are reading this like wait, did I read that right?! Yes, I was raped at the age of 17. I was very smart, but I didn't know that it wasn't my responsibility to manage or protect everyone else's emotions, so I did what I thought was protecting my family and never told anyone what happened. I was afraid that my Mom would blame herself or that my Dad and Brother would end up in jail for hurting the guy. Either way, I had an opportunity to run away, so I ran! As far away as I could and still be in the Continental U.S.. But what I didn't know was that I was running right into my destiny.

Now, I am not saying that God caused me to get hurt, because we all know that He is not that kind of God. But I can see how he allowed my hurt to carry me to where I was meant to be. The Bible talks about the iniquities of the father, and how it impacts their children. I believe this is what the devil was trying to use to cause me to run not only from California, but also from Christ. IT DIDN'T WORK! I ran to SU, found a Fellowship of Christian Athletes group and dug in. This is where my future husband sat as we read the Word together. The Word is true, Romans 8:28 says, "and we know that all things work together for good to them that love God, and to them that are called according to His purpose." Consequently, the first person I ever told was the man that God knew would eventually be my husband. I get emotional every time I tell this story because it just reminds me how much God loves us; that in my worst state, God gave me His best. The reason I am sharing this with you is because I carried this trauma with me for far too long. It hurt and eventually became very heavy and almost debilitating. I didn't recognize that letting go of this would eventually be what gave me true freedom. I recently had the opportunity to return to my childhood home and even revisited the very location where I first encountered the person that sexually assaulted me. It brought back so many emotions, but in the end I left there having chosen to walk through the difficult, almost forgotten places in my heart. I intentionally went back to some of these places, to let my body remember, to allow myself to forgive and release any negativity that I may have tried to hide. All the way down to my cells. I choose to give God glory for His love and grace. For his everlasting mercy that is displayed in my life today.

But almost more importantly, I left there having created new memories of love, an increased appreciation for wisdom and prudence, and overwhelming gratitude for God's presence through it all.

Emotional Health:

1. Are there any hidden things in your heart that are holding you back from being who God has called you to be? _____
_____
_____
_____

2. Have you been the victim of any type of trauma? Has it caused you shame, fear, or pain? What is something you can do to release those emotions today? _____
_____
_____
_____

3. Is there a sister or brother in Christ that is trustworthy enough to share this trauma with? If not that's ok, your Heavenly Father knows and is listening with an open heart. _____
_____
_____
_____

*Should you need assistance in dealing with Sexual Assault, please visit my website for a list of additional resources and recommendations for further support and healing.

Physical Health:

The emotional energy it takes to release trauma is not to be taken lightly. During the next two days, please slow down and listen to your body. You may experience cravings for things that create a sense of safety in your life. Some examples might be sweets if you naturally go toward sweets when stressed. You might feel down or depressed and want to stay in bed, or you may yearn for closeness, even intimacy. In any case, listen to what your body is telling you and give it what it needs; but in a nurturing form. Eat fruits and sweet vegetables to satisfy sweet cravings. If you feel sadness creeping in, pray, put on some worship music and allow yourself time to rest in the presence of God. If intimacy is what you need, express that need to your spouse. To be clear, sex and intimacy are not the same thing. So make sure you are not using it to hide behind what you're really in need of. If you're single, be sure that your relationships are safe should you choose to share. Healing is a very precious space; not everyone should be invited to this party.

Self Love Checklist:

Show love to yourself with these daily exercises

- Long, gentle walk, swimming or yoga
- Added Organic veggies to meal
- Drink H2O
- Talk with friends
- Deep Breathing
- Essential Oils for relaxation
- Herbal Tea
- Oil Pulling
- Spend time in nature
- Laughing
- Dancing
- Prayer

Nighttime reflection:

Today I accomplished:_____

Since I can do ALL things through Christ, tomorrow I will:

_____

_____

_____

_____

_____

_____

_____

_____

_____

_____

_____

_____

_____

_____

I'm grateful for?_____

Journal your thoughts/prayers:

_____

_____

_____

_____

_____

_____

_____

_____

_____

_____

"You can't change what you don't address."

- Nichole Thomas

Days 9 & 10

Spiritual Health: Romans 5:19-21 (NKJV) Radical Obedience

19 For as by one man's disobedience many were made sinners, so also by one Man's obedience many will be made righteous. 20 Moreover the law entered that the offense might abound. But where sin abounded, grace abounded much more, 21 so that as sin reigned in death, even so grace might reign through righteousness to eternal life through Jesus Christ our Lord.

A few days ago, I met with a sister in Christ. Having fellowship with other believers is always so encouraging and uplifting especially when their hearts are lined up with yours in pursuing God. During our conversation, I found myself talking about how within the past few years I can feel God is calling me to another level. Not so sure how, but that the "how" was none of my concern. If I'm totally honest here, I felt like I was having an out of body experience. I knew I was saying it, and I knew I genuinely felt that, but I couldn't believe it was coming out of my mouth. Me? The type "A" personality, the "control freak," the one who is always planning; yep me. Those words rolled off my tongue with such ease I laugh now just thinking about it. The amazing thing about all of this is that it's truly God's grace that has allowed me to grow into this place. Digging deeper and desiring a new level in Christ isn't for the squeamish. It requires discipline, honesty about where you are in Him, and OBEDIENCE. It actually requires RADICAL OBEDIENCE.

That's where the title of this devotion comes from. I have had so many situations in my life where God wanted something different for me. In some cases I obeyed; in others I hesitated and then obeyed. But in other ways where the ramifications of my disobedience weren't nearly as visible, I flat-out disobeyed. For instance, with my eating. I heard God very clearly say that I should check in with the Holy Spirit before I put anything that isn't a protein, fruit or vegetable into my mouth. Sometimes a food would look so good that I just wanted it. So I ate it. Not realizing that it had hidden gluten, or something else in it that would cause me significant pain, or other problems later on. I had very little discipline when it came to this, but I am so thankful for God's grace in allowing me to grow in this area every day.

Another way was dealing with my children; if one was disobedient, my husband and I would just handle it. We wouldn't always pray about how to handle it beforehand. Not understanding that some situations can come as trauma to a child and that the goal of parenting is to train them up in the way they "should" go, and not create tiny replicas of us. The last way I have come to learn to obey God's voice is with my gifts. A lot of us find ourselves depleted, exhausted, overworked and very angry at the world because we give too much of ourselves away. Knowing how to say NO to the things that God hasn't instructed us to do is just as important as when to say yes. It can save us heartache, pain, and even damaged relationships. The important thing to understand is that obedience to God is ALWAYS for our good, even when it's hard. Another thing is that God's grace is sufficient, and in our weakness, He is strong.

Emotional Health:

1. When I want to eat something I shouldn't, I've found that breathing and then praying about it helps me to make a better choice. What is something you have a hard time being obedient about? _____

_____

_____

2. How does that choice affect your body, mind and spirit? _____

_____

_____

_____

3. When you stumble and aren't obedient, how do you respond? Do you stay in it and feel awful? Or do you repent, and go after obedience again? _____

_____

_____

_____

_____

_____

_____

_____

_____

_____

_____

_____

_____

_____

Physical Health:

Over the next two days, use the Journal space in this book and write out some areas in which you may have missed God. Whether in your body, heart, mind, or with relationships, how can you honestly say you didn't choose God's way? Pay close attention to the foods you are drawn to eating during this time. Add fruits and sweet vegetables to this next two days. Most of us have difficulty with feelings of guilt, and we may reach for sweet foods, and other addictive things like caffeine or foods high in carbohydrates to lessen the discomfort. Try to avoid this by reaching for your sweet fruits and veggies and water instead. Also try adding activity that is very physical. Like boxing, kick-boxing, strength training, swimming, or Zumba. The idea is that you give yourself the space to hit, kick, punch, pull, and resist the devil in a physical way. This will help you release whatever feelings of condemnation he may be trying to throw at you that we know are a lie. You are victorious, and will win the fight.

Self Love Checklist:

Show love to yourself with these daily exercises
*
* Long, gentle walk, swimming or yoga
* Added Organic veggies to meal
* Drink H2O
* Talk with friends
* Deep Breathing
* Essential Oils for relaxation
* Herbal Tea
* Oil Pulling
* Spend time in nature
* Laughing
* Dancing
* Prayer

Nighttime reflection:

Today I accomplished:_____

Since I can do ALL things through Christ, tomorrow I will:

_____

_____

_____

I'm grateful for? _____

_____

Journal your thoughts/prayers:

_____

_____

_____

_____

_____

_____

_____

_____

_____

_____

_____

_____

_____

_____

_____

_____

_____

_____

_____

Days 11 & 12

Spiritual Health: Proverbs 4:10-13 (NKJV) Asking For Directions

10 Listen my son, accept what I say, and the years of your life will be many. *11* I instruct you in the way of wisdom and lead you along straight paths. *12* When you walk, your steps will not be hampered, when you run, you will not stumble. *13* Hold on to instruction, do not let it go; guard it well, for it is your life.

Emotional Health:

Today, I would like to ask you to do something that you might not be comfortable with. Do you have a close friend, accountability partner, or mentor? Someone you trust wholeheartedly to ask them the following questions? Please make sure you are comfortable with receiving wisdom from these people. It is a challenging exercise so choosing the right person is very important.

1) What are 2 areas I need to mature in for my relationship with God to grow?

2) How do you believe God has changed me in recent years?

3) What are my best qualities?

4) What do you think I should work on to improve physically?

Tough right? I know, but learning to receive wisdom can catapult you into your destiny.

Physical Health:

Today and tomorrow should be days of quiet reflection and meditation on the things that God has shown you through the wisdom of your mentor/accountability partner. Focus on hydration and movement. Drink as much water, herbal tea, coconut water, and organic fruit juices as possible. Also consider daily walking (outside if possible at a brisk pace. The goal is to increase circulation and elimination. Sometimes we are resistant to accepting new ideas about ourselves because we have the old ones stuck in our hearts. While keeping your body hydrated and increasing movement, you can release the toxic ideas of the past and move forward into the greatness God has designed for you!

Nighttime reflection:

Today I accomplished:_____

Since I can do ALL things through Christ, tomorrow I will:

_____

_____

_____

I'm grateful for?_____

Journal your thoughts/prayers:

_____

_____

_____

_____

_____

_____

_____

_____

_____

_____

_____

_____

_____

_____

_____

_____

_____

Ginger Tea

12 thinly sliced fresh ginger, pounded with mortar or rolling pin
2 lemons, juiced or sliced
3 cups of water
1 tbsp. raw honey

Put ginger, lemon juice and water in a small sauce pan. Bring to a boil, reduce to low heat and simmer 20-25 minutes. Add honey, strain and serve.

Days 13 & 14

Spiritual Health: Acts 13:38-39 (NKJV) You've been Forgiven

38 *Therefore let it be known to you, brethren, that through this Man is preached to you the forgiveness of sins;***39** *and by Him everyone who believes is justified from all things from which you could not be justified by the law of Moses*

When I was a little girl, I hated getting in trouble. Regardless of the reason, I hated getting in trouble. The angst and worry that loomed over my head was enough of a deterrent for me not to duplicate the offense a second time. It hurt me to my heart to see my parents look disappointed about something I had done. I also had a tender heart towards God at an early age and I never wanted to make God sad as I would often say. Fast forward 30 years to my children now. I have one that is like me, and one that seems to be the exact opposite. From the responses to doing things they know aren't right, to the posture they have when dealing with the consequences. We are just made differently, and I sometimes find myself challenged with how to respond.

One day, the child of mine who is built a little differently than I asked me why there was no consequence to the choice made earlier that day. I replied, "Because God told me to give you grace, just like He gives me, everyday." I wasn't prepared for the response. Tears began to flow, emotions were exposed and a tender heart returned. As I held my child in my arms, the conversation turned to Why God loves us so much. I answered simply, because He created us to have relationship with him, and when we are disobedient, or when we choose sin, it separates us from Him. He doesn't want to be separated from us because He loves us and wants only good for our life. That's why He sent his only Son to die for us, to forgive our sins.

As my baby looked up at me, I could sense a painful realization in those short moments.

"He died so I could be forgiven?"

"Yes, love. So all of us could be forgiven." Then my child asked,"What can I do to thank him?"

As I thought about how to answer this question in a way that a child would understand, I realized this is how God looks at us when we come to him. He looks down at us with a tender heart, and only wants us to know that He loves us and has already provided the one thing we need, His forgiveness. We have to come to understand just how powerful that is, and what it gives us access to as His children. You have been set free from sin and death. No longer does sickness, disease, fear, anger, resentment, betrayal, abandonment, worry, problems or any other thing have power over you. Divine wellness is your birthright as a believer in Christ Jesus. To answer the question, "What can we do to thank Him?" The answer is actually simple: repent and turn away from the things that makes honoring God a challenge.

Emotional Health:

1. How does God's forgiveness impact my physical health? _____
_____

2. Have I accepted God's forgiveness? Why or why not? _____
_____
_____

3. Can I forgive myself? Why or why not?_____
_____
_____
_____
_____
_____
_____
_____
_____
_____
_____
_____
_____
_____
_____
_____

Physical Health:

Forgiveness is a big concept and sometimes it's hard to break down into the many areas of our lives. For the next two days, choose activities that place you in a position to worship God. Maybe yoga, and humbly place yourself in child's pose for the entire time, or put on your favorite CD and dance around your house with hands raised in worship. If you don't have time for any of that, try taking a walk during your lunch hour as you listen to "Worth" by Anthony Brown & Group Therapy or any of your favorite songs. It doesn't matter how, just think about the sacrifice that was given so that you could be set free from every sin. Practice gratitude today.

For your food choices, add good fats to your meals. Things like coconut and olive oil, avocado, almond or peanut butter. Also think about wild caught cold water fish like salmon or sardines, flaxseed and walnuts. All of these things are filled with Omega Fatty Acids, and act as a balm to your body calming, restoring and healing areas that need it. Just like God's grace and forgiveness.

Nicki's Tips:
* Avoid corn oil, soy, partially hydrogenated oils, and non-organic meats.

Self Love Checklist:

Show love to yourself with these daily exercises

- Long, gentle walk, swimming or yoga
- Added Organic veggies to meal
- Drink H2O
- Talk with friends
- Deep Breathing
- Essential Oils for relaxation
- Herbal Tea
- Oil Pulling
- Spend time in nature
- Laughing
- Dancing
- Prayer

Nighttime reflection:

Today I accomplished:_____

Since I can do ALL things through Christ, tomorrow I will:

_____

_____

I'm grateful for?_____

Journal your thoughts/prayers:

_____

_____

_____

_____

_____

_____

_____

_____

_____

_____

_____

_____

_____

_____

_____

_____

_____

_____

_____

_____

_____

Vegan Avocado Chocolate Mousse

4 very ripe avocados
1/2 cup organic putted dates
1/4 cup organic maple syrup
1/2 cup organic unsweetened cocoa powder
1/3 cup coconut milk (full-fat)
1 tsp. organic Vanilla extract
Pinch of **Virtuous Living Himalayan Salt**

Directions:
Combine all ingredients in a food processor or blender on high speed until smooth. Pour or spoon into individual ramekins and refrigerate for at least 2 hours.

For thicker mousse, simply use less milk. Recipe can be prepared up to 1 day in advance. Garnish with toasted pistachios, fresh berries, or sliced oranges. Serve chilled.

"A merry heart doeth good like a medicine, but a broken spirit dries the bones..."

-Proverbs 17:22

Days 15 & 16

Spiritual Health: Matt 19:26 (NKJV) What can you do with God?

19 *Jesus looked at them and said, "With man this is impossible, but with God; all things are possible."*

So often we think about situations in our lives where we can remember the impossible happening. We got the job we prayed for or our child received the grade we hoped for. Even things that seemed impossible but came to pass like you speaking to thousands about your love for Christ. It all seems like a major blessing at the time, but if we're really honest, have you ever felt God didn't do it all by himself? Your son also studied really hard, and that helped him get the great grade. You were prepared for your interview for the new job, and had even researched the potential new company owner's alma mater, so that connection had to help, right? If you have ever thought this way, you are not alone. However, you and I are WRONG if we are thinking about the blessings of God in this manner. God is God, and He doesn't need our help in his ability to be omnipotent, omniscient or omnipresent. We are to change our hearts, desires and prayers so that they line up with the word of God. The word doesn't change to line up with us. Understanding this is one of the major keys to maturing in Christ, and to walking in God's will for our lives. My life began to change when I realized that I needed to line my life and thoughts up with the Word of God. He loves us so much, and desires to bless us but not to enlarge our egos; to help us see that Psalms 37:4 is true; that when we delight ourselves in him, He will give us the desires of our hearts.

So what does your heart desire? What are some things in your life that you want God to do? And how are your thoughts, desires, and ego hindering this from happening? Today, let us remember that the God that created the heavens and the Earth is the same God that desires to bless you. How can you shift your thinking to line up with the Word of God?

Emotional Health:

Answer the questions from the devotion here: _____

_____

_____

_____

_____

_____

_____

_____

_____

_____

_____

_____

_____

_____

_____

_____

_____

_____

_____

_____

_____

_____

_____

_____

_____

_____

_____

_____

_____

_____

_____

Physical Health:

For the next two days, you are going to trust God to give you the ability to prepare a meal from scratch. For some this may be easy, but for others it may give you nightmares. You have 2 options below. Feel free to modify the protein; i.e., chicken for fish, or beef for lamb to suit your needs. There are two recipes to choose from and for those that don't enjoy cooking, this may be a time to fall on your knees and ask God for extra grace to help you get through this devotion. Our bodies are so special to God, and taking the time to learn how to prepare foods that will nourish it, is an act of worship. You can do this, and I am so proud of you for walking through this with a heart to honor God and your temple.

All recipes are in the back of the book in the Original Recipe's section. Refer to these when deciding which recipes you will prepare.

Roasted Chicken, with root vegetables, mixed green salad with honey citrus vinaigrette. Herb crusted Lamb chops, roasted sweet potatoes, Mixed green salad with Nicoise vinaigrette.

Self Love Checklist:

Show love to yourself with these daily exercises

- Long, gentle walk, swimming or yoga
- Added Organic veggies to meal
- Drink H2O
- Talk with friends
- Deep Breathing
- Essential Oils for relaxation
- Herbal Tea
- Oil Pulling
- Spend time in nature
- Laughing
- Dancing
- Prayer

Nighttime reflection:

Today I accomplished:_____

Since I can do ALL things through Christ, tomorrow I will:

_____

_____

_____

_____

_____

_____

_____

_____

_____

_____

_____

_____

_____

I'm grateful for?_____

Journal your thoughts/prayers:

_____

_____

_____

_____

_____

_____

_____

_____

_____

_____

_____

_____

_____

Days 17 & 18

Spiritual Health: Matthew 11:28-30 (NKJV) Rest, Seriously?

28 *"Come unto me, all you who are weary and burdened, and I will give you rest.* **29** *Take my yoke upon you and learn from me, for I am gentle and humble in heart, and you will find rest for your souls. For my yoke is easy and my burden is light."*

For quite a long time the word "rest" was not a relatable term to me. I am the daughter of two "non-resters". I mean, these two people, my mom and dad couldn't just sit down and rest if you paid them. So needless to say, I hadn't acquired much experience resting as a young woman until I met my husband. My husband, Mr. Etan Thomas is one of the best "resters" I have ever known. I am actually laughing out loud as I write this because I used to find myself mad at him when he would say, "Ok babe, I'm gonna go take a nap." "Nap? Are you kidding me? Do you have any idea how much stuff there is to get done?" I would say. His reply would floor me every time. "Yes, I know, but I'm tired. We'll get it done." And off he'd go to take a long, relaxing, 2-hour nap.

Now I know some of you are steaming just thinking about this...but let me frame it for you. This was at a point in our life when we had the ability to structure our day in a way that was effective and less stressful. Simply put, he did that and I didn't. I thought that I needed to appear busy at all times because I was a homemaker, and I didn't want my husband to think I was lazy. The old tapes I played over and over in my head came from my childhood home, not from my husband. So I wore myself out, and eventually became very sick. Adrenal Fatigue or Chronic Fatigue Syndrome, and a whole host of other diagnoses became my life. I was finally forced to stop because my body said "NO MORE." The Holy Spirit eventually showed me that I didn't rest when I should because I had this notion that my works would please God. I thought that He would be thrilled to see a young woman working so diligently to serve her family. And because He was pleased, everything in our life would be great. WRONG! I soon learned that when I try to do things beyond my own strength, without consulting Him first, that is actually a slap in God's face. Yes, I believe He desires that I care for my family, but He also wants me to take care of the body He gave me. So if rest was good enough for Him, why not me?

I realized I had been missing it. Whether struggling because of the weight of internal or external pressures, I began to read the Word on rest. Proverbs 3 talks about wisdom, sound judgmentand discernment. Verse 24 says, "When you lie down you will not be afraid, when you lie down, your sleep will be sweet." That was exactly why I didn't rest...fear! I was afraid that things wouldn't get done, I was afraid that I would appear lazy, afraid that I would miss out on something, afraid to let others help, yada yada yada! I was in a perpetual state of fear, and who would have thought that I would discover it through an inability to rest.

Thanks be to God that I now value rest highly. I appreciate my Mom, Dad, and Mother-in-Love and their willingness to come and help us with their grand babies. I accept help, I have learned to delegate, and I have learned to say NO! All of this is giving me more opportunities to rest in the Lord, and now I take every chance I get. I am so grateful to have learned this lesson at an early stage in my life, so that God could heal and restore my body and bring it to health.

Emotional Health:

1. Are you a good "rester"? _____

_____

_____

_____

2. Why or why not? _____

_____

_____

_____

3. What do you think will change in your life if you slept better? _____

_____

_____

_____

_____

_____

_____

_____

_____

_____

_____

Physical Health:

For the next two days, I would like you to meditate on Matthew 11:28-30 and practice a sleep routine. Using lavender essential oils, add two drops to your pillow away from your eyes, before bed. Do not eat at least 2-3 hours before going to sleep. Try finding an app with sounds that relax you. I love ocean waves and they help me sleep like a baby. Pray before you go to sleep that God will give you sweet sleep and sweet dreams, and place your fears in His hands. Put on your sounds as you are ready to lie down. Drink a half a glass of room temperature water after your prayer and turn in, knowing that God loves you, and that your well-being is important to him.

Nicki's Tips:

If using a diffuser or incense, please follow the instructions carefully to prevent fire or the diffuser leaking. For more information on good quality essential oils please visit my website.

Self Love Checklist:

Show love to yourself with these daily exercises

- Long, gentle walk, swimming or yoga
- Added Organic veggies to meal
- Drink H2O
- Talk with friends
- Deep Breathing
- Essential Oils for relaxation
- Herbal Tea
- Oil Pulling
- Spend time in nature
- Laughing
- Dancing
- Prayer

Nighttime reflection:

Today I accomplished:_____

Since I can do ALL things through Christ, tomorrow I will:

_____

_____

_____

_____

I'm grateful for?_____

Journal your thoughts/prayers:

_____

_____

_____

_____

_____

_____

_____

_____

_____

_____

_____

_____

_____

_____

_____

_____

_____

_____

_____

Days 19 & 20

Spiritual Health: James 1:4 (NKJV) My Patience sucks!

4 *"But let patience have her perfect work, that ye may be perfect and entire, wanting nothing."*

So I have been writing a large portion of this book while completing a fast. The cool thing about it was that I had set a goal for myself that I would complete it by the time the fast was done. Well, as the saying goes, we plan and God laughs...and so it was. I had planned everything out to where I only had 3 devotionals to write while I was on Spring Break with my family. I thought, only 3, I can do that. Fast forward and I got absolutely nothing done on my trip. Nada, Zero, a big fat goose egg! I was frustrated when we returned to normal life and I still hadn't completed this book. I started to act strange. Disappointed in myself for not "honoring" my commitment to God, I began to act "stankily". This is my family's creation of a new word that is a combination of "stinky" and "cranky" all in one. My kids asked me what was wrong, and honestly my hubby steered clear of me for a couple of days. Then it hit me. I made this commitment; God didn't tell me to do this. I made the plans, and then asked God for grace after the fact. I made the choice to put myself on a schedule and not consider the fact that maybe God wanted me to glean something important from my experiences during our trip. Maybe those experiences would benefit someone who is reading this right now...

And here we are.

I am just like you as I write this devotion for today. I am learning everyday what James 1:4 means to "let patience have her perfect work, that I may be perfect and entire, wanting nothing." God's plan is perfect, and if we can learn to be patient in our desire to honor him, it will also serve as a way to bless others in the process. I'm learning that my heart can be in the right place, but when I choose to move at the wrong time, I may miss what God wants to develop in me.

Emotional Health:

1. Is patience something that comes easily for you? _____

_____

_____

2. What does this scripture mean to you?_____

_____

3. Do you see benefit in allowing God to develop your patience? _____

_____

_____

4. Is there one area of your life where you struggle with God on being patient? What is it and what do you sense God wants you to do to improve it?_____

_____

_____

_____

_____

_____

_____

_____

_____

_____

_____

_____

_____

_____

_____

_____

_____

_____

_____

_____

Physical Health:

Perfecting patience requires the art of being present. It means that you have an appreciation for the moment you are in RIGHT NOW! It sounds like such an easy idea, but most of our emotions come from a place of concern about the past or the future. The next two days, I would like for you to do a mental exercise 2-3 times a day; to simply be still. To think about the moment you are in, and to take every possible step to enjoy that moment. This moment is really what matters, so if you're at work, at home, with friends or by yourself, take the next minute and quiet yourself. Think about your job or career; how blessed you are to have it. Think about your friends and family; what you give to them and how you are exactly where you are supposed to be. It seems so simple but it's really one of the most difficult things to do.

Next, repeat James 1:4 to yourself. God wants us to be perfect and entire; another translation for that is whole and completely well. As for physical activity, look to add 10 minutes to your cardio routine, or simply take a long walk with a friend. As an extension of the patience exercise, try making the recipe for Risotto in the next day or so. It requires patience, but the results are amazing!

Nicki's Tips: Being present is made easier when we focus on our breathing. Try the balanced breathing technique by inhaling and exhaling for a count of 4 times each.

Self Love Checklist:

Show love to yourself with these daily exercises

- Long, gentle walk, swimming or yoga
- Added Organic veggies to meal
- Drink H2O
- Talk with friends
- Deep Breathing
- Essential Oils for relaxation
- Herbal Tea
- Oil Pulling
- Spend time in nature
- Laughing
- Dancing
- Prayer

Nighttime reflection:

Today I accomplished:_____

Since I can do ALL things through Christ, tomorrow I will:

_____
_____
_____

I'm grateful for?_____

Journal your thoughts/prayers:

_____
_____
_____
_____
_____
_____
_____
_____
_____
_____
_____
_____
_____
_____
_____
_____
_____
_____
_____
_____

Mushroom Risotto

Ingredients

1 Cup Arborio Rice
2 cups GF Chicken Stock
2 Tsp Ghee, divided
1 sweet onion, chopped
1 clove garlic, minced
1 Cups *Frey Sauvignon Blanc, or preferred dry white wine
1 1/2 cup wild mushrooms
2 Tbsp. **Virtuous Living Hope Spice blend**
1/4 cup grated Parmesan cheese

*Frey is a brand that uses Gluten & Sulfite free procedures in making its wines.

Directions:

Heat a large sauté pan to medium heat, add 2 teaspoons ghee. Add onion, cook until translucent. Add garlic, cook until fragrant, about 2 minutes. Add hope to the pan and add mushrooms, lightly sear both sides, reducing heat to mediumlow. Remove mushroom, add 1 teaspoon ghee and add dry rice to pan. Stirring gently until grains are coated in oil. Increase heat to high, add wine and bring to a boil, stirring vigorously to agitate the rice. Then reduce heat to medium and cook until wine is almost gone. Add stock, 1/2 cup at a time until absorbed, stirring constantly. Continue until all stock has been reincorporated, about 20 minutes. Add mushrooms, fold gently to incorporate, remove from heat and sprinkle parmesean cheese on top and serve.

Days 21 & 22

Spiritual Health: Proverbs 27:17 (NKJV) Intense Fellowship

17 As iron sharpens iron, so a man sharpens the countenance of his friend.

I remember hearing my Pastor and First Lady talk about "intense fellowship". It was an endearing term they used when referring to the times when they argued. My husband and I have chosen to adopt that term for ourselves. One day, when I woke up on the side of the bed that seemed to have been reserved for the devil himself (usually only happens after I've ingested gluten accidentally) I found myself in a very odd place. I felt overwhelmed with emotion, frusrated and angry at someone in my family. My husband asked me what was wrong, and if I was OK. As I considered how I would answer these questions, I felt myself getting more and more upset. As I was about to respond I said to myself, "Careful, remember he isn't the one you're upset with." So I simply told him that I wasn't really ok, but that I was choosing to place my heart, hurt feelings and fears in God's hands and trust Him to work it out.

Not long after that conversation with my hubby God provided an opportunity for me to share my heart and my love with the person I was unhappy with. Then God told me to tell the "Truth in Love" and apologize if that hadn't been accomplished. Of course apologizing to someone you feel you haven't wronged can be difficult, but as an act of obedience to God I knew I needed to bite the bullet. I chose to obey, and oh how God showed out in my life.

I am so glad to have a chance to see God's hand in my life; to watch the miracles he performs when we choose to obey. I told the truth, apologized, and did it all in love because Christ gave me the power to. His grace really does give us what we need to overcome all obstacles.

Emotional Health:

1. Do you tend to avoid confrontation or run to it? _____

_____

2. Is it harmful to your relationships to hold your feelings in? _____

_____

_____

3. Do you feel that holding on to your feelings, i.e., anger, frustration, resentment are keeping you in a position of power in your relationships? _____

_____

4. Do you trust God enough to let go of those feelings that are no longer serving you? _____

_____

_____

Physical Health:

Intense fellowship doesn't have to be a bad thing. Sometimes great things come out of deep heartfelt conversations where you are completely transparent and vulnerable. The trick is to know your audience. Don't share your feelings with someone who doesn't have your best interests at heart. If there is tension or strife from a particular event, always pray about how to address your concerns. I've found that when I release control of that situation through prayer, God prepares the person's heart to receive what I have to say. For the next two days, I would like you to make time to meet a friend for tea. Have a conversation that might be a little deeper than the surface. If this is a close friend, share with them what you are doing and feel free to really work on your friendship. The fruit of this type of exercise is helpful in developing good relationships, but also to know which relationships might have run their course.

Self Love Checklist:

Show love to yourself with these daily exercises

- Long, gentle walk, swimming or yoga
- Added Organic veggies to meal
- Drink H2O
- Talk with friends
- Deep Breathing
- Essential Oils for relaxation
- Herbal Tea
- Oil Pulling
- Spend time in nature
- Laughing
- Dancing
- Prayer

Nighttime reflection:

Today I accomplished:_____

Since I can do ALL things through Christ, tomorrow I will:

_____

_____

_____

I'm grateful for?_____

Journal your thoughts/prayers:

_____

_____

_____

_____

_____

_____

_____

_____

_____

_____

_____

_____

_____

_____

_____

_____

_____

_____

"Hydrate often"

\- Nichole Thomas

Days 23 & 24

Spiritual Health: *Ecclesiastes 11:1-8 (NKJV)* **Diligence and Grace**

1 Cast your bread upon the waters, for you will find it after many days. 2 Give a serving to seven, and also to eight, for you do not know what evil will be on the earth. *3* If the clouds are full of rain, they empty themselves upon the earth; and if a tree falls to the south or the north, in the place where the tree falls, there it shall lie.

4 He who observes the wind will not sow, and he who regards the clouds will not reap. *5* As you do not know what is the way of the wind, or how the bones grow in the womb of her who is with child, so you do not know the works of God who makes everything.

6 In the morning sow your seed, and in the evening do not withhold your hand; for you do not know which will prosper, either this or that, or whether both alike will be good. *7* Truly the light is sweet, and it is pleasant for the eyes to behold the sun; *8* but if a man lives many years and rejoices in them all, yet let him remember the days of darkness, for they will be many. All that is coming is vanity.

When we stay fixated on only the bad things that have happened in our lives, we lose the value of the experience, and lose an opportunity for growth. While it's very important to know where your heart and mind are and stay present, we must do so remembering His presence, and that gives us hope in Christ to move forward. The scripture says he who observes the wind, will not sow. Similarly, he who continues to relive the pains of the past, will be robbed of joy in life. Although sowing and reaping are natural laws, sometimes all it takes is for us to become fixated on the wind and its potential to harm our seed, and wemiss an opportunity for a blessing.

Choose to stay diligent in all things. Choose to remind yourself that we are ALL a work in progress. Choose to be aware of your flaws, and commit to working on them, and growing in grace and love for yourself. Also seek more love and grace from your heavenly Father. Choose diligence to gain peace, and a way that does not allow the enemy to steal another second of joy or peace from you! You are who God loves and sees as worth every drop of blood that Jesus shed on the Cross. You are precious.

Emotional Health

1. When problems come, do you tend to believe they are a punishment for something you've done? _____

_____

_____

2. What do you think God believes about you? _____

_____

_____

_____

3. Do you show yourself grace? How? _____

_____

_____

_____

_____

_____

_____

_____

_____

_____

_____

_____

_____

_____

_____

_____

_____

_____

_____

_____

_____

Physical Health

Exercise faith by writing down 3 things that you are in Christ! Are you free, happy, bold or courageous? Do you believe that? If you do, thank God and move on to writing three things that you may struggle to believe.

Repeat the things that you are in Christ daily for the next couple of days. Post a note card on your mirror and remind yourself throughout the day. You are planting seeds of faith into your heart, and you will reap a harvest if you don't quit.

Self Love Checklist:

Show love to yourself with these daily exercises

- Long, gentle walk, swimming or yoga
- Added Organic veggies to meal
- Drink H2O
- Talk with friends
- Deep Breathing
- Essential Oils for relaxation
- Herbal Tea
- Oil Pulling
- Spend time in nature
- Laughing
- Dancing
- Prayer

Nighttime reflection:

Today I accomplished:_____

Since I can do ALL things through Christ, tomorrow I will:

_____

I'm grateful for?_____

Journal your thoughts/prayers:

_____

_____

_____

_____

_____

_____

_____

_____

_____

_____

_____

_____

_____

_____

_____

_____

_____

_____

_____

_____

_____

_____

_____

_____

"Life expectancy would grow by leaps and bounds if green vegetables smelled as good as bacon"

- Doug Larson

Days 25 & 26

Spiritual Health: *Psalms 139:13-14 (NKJV **Shine Bright Like a Diamond***

13 But let patience have her perfect work, that ye may be perfect and entire, wanting nothing.

14 will praise You, for I am fearfully and wonderfully made; Marvelous are Your works, And that my soul knows very well.

Have you ever felt like you didn't fit in? Like you don't have that thing that you may see in others? Have you ever questioned if what God put in your heart to do, is too big? If the answer to any of those questions is yes, then this is for you!

This was me. My whole life felt like one big experiment in "fitting out". From being taller than 90% of my classmates, to being the only girl to play on certain basketball teams. To loving God so much from an early age that I would go against the grain in most social settings because of my convictions. To the times where the call on my life felt like it was just too much. I have shed so many tears in my lifetime because I didn't understand who God made me to be and exactly what He made me for. I finally started to realize...I didn't fit in. But then again, I was never designed to.

There comes a time in a persons life when we must recognize God does have his hand on us. Your life is not only to be a living witness of his grace, but also of the love and intentionality with which you were created! You are truly something special! And He formed and fashioned you, and created you to walk in your divine purpose! So as you think about that today, look at yourself, and find the places where you hide, or shrink back. Remember whose you are and how special you are to God, and to me, and move. You don't fit in because you weren't designed to! You stand out because you're a star. Stars don't stop shining because another is shining next to them. The light inside of you for the things you are designed for, must come from you. When I focus on your light, and start to lean in your direction, all I do is cast a shadow. That's not what God wants for us.

Being you, authentically, bravely, and wonderfully, is EXACTLY who you are supposed to be. If your dreams don't scare you, they're not big enough!

Emotional Health

1. What has God given you a passion for? _____
_____
_____
_____
_____

2. Do your dreams scare you? Why or why not?
_____
_____

Journal your dreams in the blank pages provided. This can be however it comes out for you. Sketches, flow charts, lists, doodles...whatever gets your wheels turning! Write the vision and make it plain.

_____
_____
_____
_____
_____
_____
_____
_____
_____
_____
_____
_____
_____
_____
_____
_____
_____
_____

Physical Health:

For the next two days, I'd like for you to focus on what you've written down. Write and be specific about what your life looks like in 1, 3, and 5 years. After you've completed this, take your pages and pray over them. Offer those dreams and desires back to the one who created you. Then choose one dream to share with a prayer partner, friend or loved one. When doing this, speak boldly, as if it's already done.

Exercises that are helpful during this process are group classes. Zumba, aerobics, body pump, or even Cross-fit! Remind yourself while working out that although you are working hard, having the support of others in this group is what will make the dream work. We are all important to Him, but in order to see our dreams come to pass, it is going to take the right relationships.

Self Love Checklist:

Show love to yourself with these daily exercises

- Long, gentle walk, swimming or yoga
- Added Organic veggies to meal
- Drink H2O
- Talk with friends
- Deep Breathing
- Essential Oils for relaxation
- Herbal Tea
- Oil Pulling
- Spend time in nature
- Laughing
- Dancing
- Prayer

Nighttime reflection:

Today I accomplished:_____

Since I can do ALL things through Christ, tomorrow I will:

_____

_____

_____

_____

I'm grateful for?_____

Journal your thoughts/prayers:

_____

_____

_____

_____

_____

_____

_____

_____

_____

_____

_____

_____

_____

_____

_____

_____

_____

_____

_____

_____

"Loving ourselves through the process of owning our story is the bravest thing we'll ever do"

-Dr. Brene Brown

Days 27 & 28

Spiritual Health: *1 Peter 5:8 (NKJV)* ***Houston, we have a problem***

8 *Be sober, be vigilant; because your adversary the devil walks about like a roaring lion, seeking whom he may devour.*

There was a time when it seemed like all hell had broken loose in my life! I was different though. Almost like I anticipated the attack of the enemy and was ready to withstand it. You'd think that was a great thing, right? A great posture to have when it comes to standing firm.

Well, I soon came to learn that because of the frequency of those attacks, I had begun to expect them! I had a certainty about their impending nature and had adopted a pose in their anticipation. The Holy Spirit gently showed me that I was more expectant of the enemy, than of the power of God to show up in my life. I had trained my body, soul and mind to focus more on the tricks and traps of the enemy, than on God's ability to deliver me from them.

So I put it to the test! When my kids went out to play, I forced myself to expect them to come in without having had any incidents. When servicemen came to our house to do work, I forced myself to think on things that are good, noble, and of a good report. That they wouldn't find anything damaged or broken, only things in need of regular maintenance. And guess what happened....The attacks ceased!

The word says "your enemy, the devil walks around LIKE a roaring lion!" This word "like" is such a huge deal because it lets us know that he isn't really a threat. He walks around like one, posing, and pretending to be something he's not. He isn't capable of coming against our heavenly father so he knows he has to trick us into believing his lies. We then focus on him and do the dirty work for him! When we allow the enemy to dictate our thought life, or when we don't take the time to formulate constructive thoughts, we give him permission to wreak havoc in our lives. He seeks, or actively pursues those he may devour! He first has to have access, and that access comes from sin. So the next time you find yourself being knocked up-side the head in life, ask yourself, how might he have gained access? Repent, and quickly shift your focus back on Jesus Christ, the redeemer of your soul! You are valuable to God! Don't allow the enemy to devour you another minute of life from you.

Emotional Health:

1. Identify any areas where you have given the enemy access into your life. List them below.

_____

_____

2. Determine today, what you will shift your heart to. What has God already done that you can focus on? _____

_____

_____

3. Do you need to repent or apologize to anyone? _____

_____

_____

_____

_____

_____

_____

_____

_____

_____

_____

_____

_____

_____

_____

_____

_____

_____

_____

_____

_____

_____

Physical Health:

For the next two days, ask God to show you how you have allowed the enemy to steal your focus! Look for areas that are gateways for the enemy. It can be anything from unforgiveness to food to music, to movies. Write down these things and take them before the Father. Af-ter you ask for forgiveness, actively pursue those that need your forgiveness. Sched-ule calls or meetings to get those things right. If it's not possible to meet, or talk, just offer up a prayer for that relationship, acknowledging the areas where you may have missed it. Then know that as 1 Corinthians 10:13 says, "...God is a faithful...," and will lovingly cover and guide you into your destiny.

Self Love Checklist:

Show love to yourself with these daily exercises

- Long, gentle walk, swimming or yoga
- Added Organic veggies to meal
- Drink H2O
- Talk with friends
- Deep Breathing
- Essential Oils for relaxation
- Herbal Tea
- Oil Pulling
- Spend time in nature
- Laughing
- Dancing
- Prayer

Nighttime reflection:

Today I accomplished:_____

Since I can do ALL things through Christ, tomorrow I will:

_____

_____

_____

_____

I'm grateful for?_____

_____

Journal your thoughts/prayers:

_____

_____

_____

_____

_____

_____

_____

_____

_____

_____

_____

_____

_____

_____

_____

_____

_____

_____

Days 29 & 30

Spiritual Health: *Romans 9:31-33 (NKJV)* **The intersection of Vulnerability & Faith**

31 but the people of Israel, who pursued the law as the way of righteousness, have not attained their goal. 32 Why not? Because they pursued it not by faith but as if it were by works. They stumbled over the stumbling stone. 33 As it is written: "See, I lay in Zion a stone that causes people to stumble and a rock that makes them fall, and the one who believes in him will never be put to shame."

Not long ago, I experienced a very uncomfortable situation. I had a chance to be a part of something that I was thrilled about, but one person in charge of the event wasn't one of my biggest fans. They were the kind that smile when they see me, but scowl and twist the knife they'd like to stick in my back as I walked away. Needless to say, they were not excited to see me thrive in this new space. I'll be honest; I know some people don't know me and some simply may not like me, but that isn't my business, as long as I do what God has called me to do and walk in love. As I prayed about whether to go after this, God said to me "put yourself out there and trust me"! So that's just what I did.

I sent an email, asking if there was an opening for what I wanted to contribute, stating my qualifications and my heart to help. I knew in my heart that the answer would be no even before I sent the email, but God wanted me to learn something that day!

About an hour later I received a response saying, unfortunately, they were unable to accommodate my request, but that they would keep me in mind for next year. I was so mad. Not angry mad, but embarrassed mad, annoyed mad, and more than anything....mad that I had put myself out there!

So as I sat there reading the email, I felt this rush of emotions come over me. It was fear. Why had God allowed me to be made a fool of when I was trying my best to be obedient? I prayed and asked that very question, and learned quickly what He purposed for me. It was that I needed to understand that being vulnerable and open to the things He has for me doesn't always mean it's for right now. But to truly be vulnerable, allowing others (even those that might dislike you) to see who you are, or see you fail, allows Him to receive the glory in our lives when we triumph.

That was a hard pill for me to swallow, but I got the point. Putting up a front, and not allowing hurt, fear, or pride to stop you from being obedient may seem easier, but it's exactly that fearless "heart work" that allows God to move you into the next stage of your life because it requires faith. Faith in the sovereignty of God, Faith in the timing of God, and Faith that the vision He has placed in you will come to pass, in due season. Oh, and not long after all that another opportunity came for me to shine!

Emotional Health:

1. Is being vulnerable an easy thing for you? _____
_____
_____
_____

2. Why or why not? _____
_____
_____

3. What is the benefit of vulnerability in your personal life? _____
_____
_____
_____
_____
_____
_____
_____
_____
_____
_____
_____
_____

Physical Health:

Take a chance today; whether a new workout, trying a new recipe from the back of this book, or engaging someone you are in relationship with to deepen the connection. Pray about which step to take and then commit to being open to the entire process. Watch and see what God will do in your heart as you allow Him to expand it. Expansion always makes room for abundance.

Self Love Checklist:

Show love to yourself with these daily exercises

- Long, gentle walk, swimming or yoga
- Added Organic veggies to meal
- Drink H2O
- Talk with friends
- Deep Breathing
- Essential Oils for relaxation
- Herbal Tea
- Oil Pulling
- Spend time in nature
- Laughing
- Dancing
- Prayer

Nighttime reflection:

Today I accomplished:_____

Since I can do ALL things through Christ, tomorrow I will:

_____

_____

_____

I'm grateful for? _____

_____

_____

Journal your thoughts/prayers:

_____

_____

_____

_____

_____

_____

_____

_____

_____

_____

_____

_____

_____

_____

_____

_____

_____

_____

_____

Days 31

Spiritual Health: 1 Corinthians 16:13 & 14 (NKJV) You did it!

13Watch, stand fast in the faith, be brave, be strong. 14 Let all that you do be done with love.

Can you believe it? You made it through a full month of actively pursuing your health. Your decision to glorify God in your spirit, mind and body will impact your life for years to come. I am so amazingly proud of you and what you've accomplished.

For the last day, I would like for you to journal your thoughts and feelings about this process, if you feel this book has impacted you, how you view your body as a result, and what you plan to do moving forward to continue to take care of YOU! Also celebrate with friends or family as you have accomplished something really wonderful.

This process isn't easy, and we've only skimmed the surface but the work you've done will produce a harvest in your life. Learning to work through the matters of the heart, balancing them with scripture, choosing foods that nourish your body, and moving forward in faith is what this book is really all about. You are in a space that very few people dare to go, simply because it's uncomfortable. Growth happens when we dare to get comfortable in "un-comfortability" and allow God to develop and change us.

Since you have completed the process, you know how it would affect other people in your life, and I would love for you to share your testimonies with me and with as many people as you can. God wants us all to be healthy and well, Living Virtuously and inspiring others to do the same. So thank you for being a part of sharing and spreading LOVE!

XO,

Nichole

Congratulations

"If you can't pronounce it, don't eat it!"

- Nichole Thomas

Original Recipes

HERB / SPICE	HEALTH BENEFIT
HIMALAYAN PINK SALT (FYI: Table salt contains chemicals <u>and</u> sometimes sugar! It's void of nutritional value)	• Controls water levels within the body • Promotes a stable pH balance in the cells, including the brain • Promotes good blood sugar health • Promotes increased absorption of food elements within the digestive tract • Promotes healthy sleep patterns • Prevents cellulite • Aids vascular health
BLACK PEPPER	• Stimulates taste buds which aids digestion • Helps break up mucous congestion • Its active ingredient, piperine, has natural anti-inflammatory effects • Boosts fat metabolism, aiding in weight loss
GARLIC	• Reduces Cholesterol • Natural Aphrodisiac • Antioxidant • Plays a role in treating heart disease & stroke • Natural Antibiotic
ROSEMARY	• It's ingredient, carnosol helps prevent cancer • Improves Memory • Elevates mood • Natural Migraine Remedy • Anti-Inflammatory • Immune Booster • Antibacterial • Stimulates Hair Growth • Improves Circulation • Mild Diuretic • Liver Detoxifier • Anti-aging
CINNAMON	• Anti-Clotting • Arthritis Relief • Natural food preservative (inhibits bacterial growth and food spoilage) • Brain Health • Fights E. Coli bacteria in unpasteurized juice • Great source of fiber, iron, calcium & manganese
RAW CANE SUGAR	• Less processed and refined
VANILLA BEAN	• Contains small amounts of B-complex groups, which help in enzyme synthesis, nervous system function and regulating body metabolism • Helps relieve nausea (calms stomach) • Reduces stress
DEHYDRATED ONION	• Aids in cardiovascular health • Prevents growth of cancerous tumors • Anti-inflammatory properties • Contains calcium • Contains potassium, which helps regulate blood pressure

Breakfast

Berry Superfood Smoothie

Ingredients:
1 cup organic milk of your choice (I use goat milk)
2 cups organic berries (raspberries, blackberries, strawberries, cherries, blueberries), fresh or frozen
2 Tbsp. hemp seeds
2 tsp. lucuma powder
½ Tbsp. maca powder
1 Tbsp. vegan protein powder (I love ID Life vegan protein powder)
2 Tbsp. almond butter
½ Tbsp. raw honey (or maple syrup)

Directions:
In high-speed blender or food processor, blend all ingredients until smooth and serve.

Peanut Butter, Banana, Chia smoothie

Ingredients:
1 frozen banana
2 Tbsp ground GF flax seed
2 Tbsp powdered peanut butter
1 cup Greek yogurt, such as Fage'
1 tbsp chia seeds
1/4 cup organic Goat milk
1 1/2 tsp **Virtuous Living Faith** spice

Directions:
In high-speed blender or food processor, blend all ingredients until smooth, and serve.

Cinnamon Blueberry Quinoa Porridge

Ingredients:
2 cups organic milk (or milk of your choice)
1 cup quinoa
2Tbsp **Virtuous Living Faith** spice
1 tsp lemon zest
3 Tbsp. coconut palm sugar, monkfruit sweetner or maple syrup

Nicki's Tips - To speed the cooking time of quinoa and to remove some of the phytic acid and bitterness released when cooking, soak quinoa overnight. Quinoa naturally produces Phytic acid. Phytic acid, when not released by soaking, binds to minerals in the gut and can contribute to deficiency. The more Phytic acid you consume the more vitamin and mineral deficient one may become.

Directions:
In saucepan, combine milk and soaked quinoa; heat over medium heat, stirring in Faith or the sweeter of your choice. Slowly bring mixture to a light boil, then increase heat to create a strong boil. Let boil for 1 minute, then reduce heat to low and simmer for about 5 minutes or until quinoa is tender. Stir in lemon zest. Serve topped with fresh blueberries, nuts and banana.

Juicing Recipes
Each recipe makes 64 ounces of juice.

Mrs. Green Jeans - This is simply to detoxify the system and bring back a slight increase of alkalinity. Also a great source of B vitamins

4 apples, cored
2-3 cucumbers
Handful of parsley
2 handfuls of spinach
2 stalks of kale
1 bunch of celery
1 lemon
1 tsp. fresh ginger

Guts & Glory - This juice is perfect to help with hydration and elimination. These two things can contribute to healing in the gut, which studies show is often a necessary foundation for great health. High in Vitamin C, it is also an immune booster.

10 pieces of beets (if packaged, make sure their organic)
1 bunch of celery
1 handful cilantro
1 tsp. fresh ginger
1 cucumber
2 lemons
10 romaine lettuce leaves
1 handful of spinach
15 carrots

Big Red - A support system for you kidneys and liver, this beautiful crimson nectar helps your body by reducing the amount of toxins in your blood. It also acts as a toner for the nervous system. This juice is rich in potassium, magnesium, vitamin C, and iron.

6 apples, cored and seeded
10 pieces of beets (if packaged, make sure their organic)
1 bunch of celery
1 handful cilantro
1 cucumber
1 lemon
2 tomatoes
15 carrots

The Classic French Omelette

Ingredients:
2 organic, or pastured eggs
2 tbsp water
pinch **Virtuous Living Himalaya Pink Salt**
1 tsp **Virtuous Living Hope** spice
1 tsp ghee or butter

* Should you choose to add ingredients to your omelette, use 1/3 cup to suit this recipe

Directions:
Beat eggs well with a fork and add salt, herbs and water until blended. Heat a small skillet on medium heat and and add 1 pat (1/4 tbsp) butter to the pan. Coat pan thoroughly with butter by lifting the pan slightly, and tilting. Gently pour in the egg mixture. You will notice the edges begin to set immediately.

Gently move the cooked edges with a small silicone spatula or wooden spoon to the center and tilt allowing the uncooked parts to reach the pan. Keep cooking the egg mixture, tilting the pan gently as needed.

When the top of the eggs surface is set, and no liquid appears, flip the omelette over. (If you are not comfortable doing this, feel free to use a spatula to help you). Finish by adding your filling to one side of the omelette. Gently fold the empty side over the other covering the added ingredients. turn off the burner and lift your pan over your plate. Allow the omlette to slide out onto the plate. Garnish with fresh seasonal herbs and cracked black pepper and serve.

Fruit Infused waters

1) Pear + Raspberry + Rosemary = Lowers blood pressure, supports immune function, increases blood flow to the brain.

2) Pomegranate seeds + Persimmon + Orange + Cinnamon Sticks + Allspice Berries = Regulates blood sugar, provides antioxidants

3) Blueberries + Lemon + Cucumber = Balanced pH, detoxification, boost metabolism

4) Orange + Vanilla beans + Cinnamon Sticks = Vitamin C booster, regulate blood sugar, calming

5) Cranberries + Apple + Lemon + Orange Zest + Pomegranate Seeds = Detoxification, protect brain cells, lower bad cholesterol

Sage Maple Breakfast Sausage

Ingredients:
3 tbsp organic butter or Ghee

1 lb. ground turkey

1 lb. ground bison

1 onion, chopped

1 clove fresh garlic, chopped

1 small organic Apple, honey crisp or Granny Smith, peeled, cores and chopped

1 Tbsp **Virtuous Living's Hope** spice

1 cup of fresh sage, minced or 1 Tbsp dried sage

2 tsp maple syrup

2 tbsp **Virtuous Livings Himalayan Pink Salt**

cracked black pepper to taste

Directions
Preheat your oven to 350*

In a large skillet, melt butter or ghee. Add onions, salt and sauté until tender. Next add garlic and cook only until fragrant. Add apples cooking with onions and garlic until softened and slightly golden. Remove from heat and place in a separate bowl.

In a large mixing bowl, mix ground turkey, ground bison, herbs, spices, salt, and your sautéed ingredients together. Mix thoroughly incorporating all the ingredients. Be careful not to use metal utensils for this, as it can cause your meat to toughen. Add maple syrup and mix again.

Using a scoop or your hands, form patties and place them on a oiled baking sheet. Once all the patties are formed and placed, bake for 20-30 minutes. Be sure they are cooked through.

Serve with pastured eggs, or whole grain Gluten-free English muffins and jam.

Nicki's Tips:
Baking sausages on a cookie sheet can cut the amount of fat in your dish. Also avoid lining your baking sheets with aluminum foil. It's toxic!

Dinner & Sides

Quinoa Tabouli

Ingredients:
1 cup quinoa, thoroughly soaked, rinsed and drained in fine mesh strainer
1 cup water
2 tsp **Virtuous Livings Himalayan Pink Salt**, optional
1 sliced or chopped cucumber
1/2 cup chopped fresh shallots
1/4 cup chopped fresh mint
1/4 cup chopped parsley

Dressing:
Juice of several lemons
extra-virgin olive Oil
Virtuous Livings Himalayan Pink Salt
fresh cracked black pepper

Directions:

Bring soaked, rinsed and drained quinoa to a boil with water and salt. Cover and reduce to low heat. Cook for 10-12 minutes until water has absorbed. Turn off heat.
Fluff quinoa with a fork or spoon and transfer to bowl.

Meanwhile, make lemon vinaigrette by combining lemon juice, olive oil and salt to taste (essentially, 2 parts juice to one part oil). Combine all ingredients and refrigerate salad until chilled.

Salmon Salad Nicoise

Salad Ingredients:
mixed greens, washed and pat dry
red onion, thinly sliced
4 eggs, hard boiled, quartered
1 pint cherry tomatoes, halved
Fresh dill, chopped
Greek or Nicoise' olives, pitted
Haricot-Vert or French green beans, trimmed and chopped
1 lb. new potatoes, boiled and slightly salted, chopped
Virtuous Living Himalayan Pink Salt

Dressing:
1/2 cup red wine vinegar
1/2 cup olive oil
1tsp whole grain dijon mustard
1 small shallot, diced
1 pinch **Virtuous Living Himalayan Pink Salt**
cracked black pepper

Make the dressing:
Whisk together the vinegar, shallots, mustard, salt and pepper until thoroughly combined. Pouring slowly, add the olive oil to the mixture, whisking constantly until emulsified. Set aside

Place potatoes into a pot of cold water covering by 1 inch. Season the water with salt, and bring to a boil. Cook for 8-10 minutes, then gently add eggs to the same boiling water. Check that potatoes are tender, and turn off heat. Eggs need about 8-10 minutes for a good hard boil. If you prefer a softer boiled egg, this is the rule of thumb:
Soft boiled: 4-5 minutes
Medium: 7-8 minutes
Hard: 8-10 minutes

Remove from heat, drain your potatoes and eggs carefully in a strainer and rinse thoroughly with cold water. This will stop the cooking process. While potatoes and eggs cool, place green beans in a small skillet and sauté with 1tbsp ghee or coconut oil and 1 tsp of salt. Cook until tender and remove from heat and set aside.

Salmon FlIets

2-4 filets, wild caught, Non-GMO salmon
1 tbsp. **Virtuous Living Hope** spice
1/4 cup lemon or lime juice
2 tbsp. ghee, or coconut oil

Clean salmon by wiping gently with a damp paper towel, making sure to remove all bones. Season salmon with lemon or lime juice, Hope spice and a pinch Himalayan salt. (Feel free to leave out the salt if watching blood pressure. The acidity from the lemon will be enough) Heat a skillet on medium heat, add ghee or coconut oil. Carefully add salmon, skin side down. Allow the salmon to cook about 1 minutes. Using a spatula, carefully flip your salmon, and repeat, cooking for a total of 3 1/2 minutes. (time based on a 4 oz. fillet) Once your salmon is thoroughly cooked, remove from heat and set aside.

Plating your salad

On a platter, place green beans, potatoes sliced 1/3 inch thick, cherry tomatoes, sliced red onions, mixed greens, eggs sliced into quarters, and olives in whatever fashion you'd like. This is a very hearty salad, so you won't need to fill your plate. Drizzle with dressing and top with salmon filet.

Add a little more dressing, and freshly ground black pepper and serve.

This salad pairs nicely with a balanced Sauvignon Blanc.

Thai Turkey Stir Fry w/ Fresh Basil & Peppers

Ingredients:
1 lb. ground Turkey

1 yellow onion, sliced

1 red bell pepper, sliced

1 yellow bell pepper, sliced

2 - 3 garlic cloves, sliced to flavor oil

1 - 2 cup Fresh basil, chopped

Directions:
In a large frying pan or Wok, heat the pan over high heat for about 1 minute. Add coconut oil, and fresh sliced garlic. Remove the garlic when golden brown. Add sauce and integrate with the oil thoroughly. Add ground turkey to the sauce and cook until brown. Add veggies and cook until vegetables are tender. Remove from heat and serve over rice or in lettuce cups if you want to reduce your carbohydrates intake.

Stir Fry Sauce

Ingredients:
2/3 cup cilantro

2/3 cup parsley

2/3 cup basil or Thai basil

2 cloves garlic, peeled and chopped

2 Tbsp ginger, peeled and chopped

1/2 Tbsp red pepper flakes

1 Tbsp **Virtuous Living's Hope spice**

2 Tbsp fresh lime juice

1 Tbsp GF fish sauce

2 Tbsp of virgin coconut oil, Melted

1 Tbsp raw honey

1 pinch (1/8 **Virtuous Living Himalayan Pink Salt**)

Directions:
Whisk in all liquid ingredients, add spices, herbs, ginger and honey. Whisk together thoroughly and a pinch of salt. Set aside.

Roasted Cauliflower with Pumpkin Seeds

Ingredients:

1 head cauliflower, stems and florets

1 bunch kale, stems removed

1/4 cup toasted pumpkin seeds

1 Tbsp. organic olive oil

1 clove garlic, minced

1 onion, chopped

1 Tbsp **Virtuous Living Love** spice

1 tsp **Virtuous Living Hope** spice

Juice of ½ lemon

Directions:

Preheat your oven to 375*

On a cutting board, cut one large head of Cauliflower into quarters. Wash, pat dry and set aside in a roasting pan or deep baking dish. In a sauté pan, heat onion, garlic, olive oil and lemon juice. Add kale and cook until slightly wilted.

Pour garlic, onion, oil and kale onto cauliflower and season with **Virtuous Living Love** spice blend. Bake for approximately 25 minutes. Garnish with roasted pumpkin seeds.

Gluten Free Penne with Chicken & Lemon Sauce

Ingredients:

½ to ¾ lb. gluten-free penne pasta

1 bunch swiss chard, shredded (stems removed and diced*

2 cloves garlic, minced

1 onion, thinly sliced

2 Tbsp. extra-virgin olive oil

1 Tbsp. **Virtuous Living Hope** spice

2 Tbsp. lemon juice

Zest of 1 lemon

1/3 cup goat milk or coconut milk

1 tsp. dried (or fresh) thyme

2 tsp. **Virtuous Living Himalayan Pink salt**

¼ tsp. ground nutmeg

1 cup, chopped leftover chicken

freshly ground pepper, to taste

**Spinach or kale may be substituted for Swiss chard or collard greens for extra Vitamin C, and vitamin K.

Directions:

Cook pasta according to package directions. To make lemon sauce, combine lemon juice, lemon zest, goat milk, thyme, nutmeg, salt and pepper in a sauce pan, whisk on medium-low heat until smooth. To make Swiss chard, heat oil over medium heat in large saucepan. Stir in chard stems, garlic and onion and sauté for about 6-8 minutes, until softened and until leaves are wilted.

In large pot, combine pasta, chicken, sauce and greens. Cook over medium heat, stirring often, until heated evenly. Serve topped with freshly ground black pepper and chopped parsley. Add leftover Chicken and combine. Plate and serve.

**Use caution when eating dark green, leafy vegetables often, if you take Potassium or Magnesium medication. They may create an imbalance. Remember food is medicine, and can interact with certain medications.

Nicki's Famous Herb Crusted Lamb Chops

Ingredients:
6-8 organic, grass-fed lamb chops
2 tbsp organic grapeseed oil, divided
1/2 cup full bodied red wine
Virtuous Living Love spice
freshly cracked black pepper
6-8 cloves of garlic
10-12 fresh rosemary sprigs, leaves removed
fresh thyme

Directions:
Preheat oven to 325*.

In a food processor, gently pulse garlic, rosemary, thyme, grapeseed oil and pepper. Season lamb chops with salt on both sides. Coat each lamb chop with the herb paste completely over both sides. Heat a sauté pan to medium-high heat. Add 1 tbsp coconut oil to pan, and sear one side of your lamb chops for about 2 minutes. Try not to bother the lamb chop so that it gets a good sear, and the herb crust doesn't come off of the meat. Repeat for 1 minute on the other side and remove from heat. Allow chops to rest 2 minutes before placing them on a baking sheet to finish for another 6-8 minutes in the oven.

Using the same sauté pan, keep the remaining oil, and browned bits in the pan. Heat the pan to medium-high heat and add 1/2 cup of red wine to deglaze. Add 1 tsp. organic butter and stir. Allow the sauce to reduce by half. Add 1 sprig of thyme, and 1 sprig of rosemary to the sauce to infuse the sauce with the same "herby" goodness, and remove from heat.

Remove lamb chops from the oven, and let rest for 5 minutes. Serve with roasted potatoes, and a salad or any other green vegetable you like.

Roasted Sweet Potatoes

Ingredients:
3 to 4 medium sized sweet potatoes, cut into wedges
Virtuous Living Himalayan Pink Salt, to taste
coconut oil
juice of 1 lemon
5-8 fresh rosemary sprigs

Directions:
Preheat oven to 350* F. Lightly coat baking sheet with coconut oil. In a large bowl, toss sweet potato wedges with remaining ingredients, making sure to coat evenly with evenly seasoning. Place wedges on baking sheet and bake for 20 minutes or until desired crispiness.

Serve along side grilled T-bone steak for a fun turn on Steak Frites, the healthier way.

* If someone is allergic to lemons, you can always use lime or even a splash of apple cider vinegar for a tangy twist.

Seasonal Root Veggie Medley

Ingredients:
rainbow carrots, halved or quartered, length wise
parsnips, halved or quartered, length wise
brussell sprouts, halved
onions, halved or quartered, length wise
organic ooconut olive oil or non-GMO grapeseed oil
freshly ground pepper
juice of ½ or 1 lemon
fresh parsley
2 Tbsp **Virtuous Living Hope** spice

Dressing:
Preheat oven to 350* F. Generously coat vegetables in oil, lemon juice, pepper and spices (if desired) and arrange in single layer in roasting pan or baking sheet. Bake vegetables for 30 to 45 minutes. Enjoy as a side dish or add to salads, and pilafs.

Gluten-Free Creole Crab Cakes

Ingredients:

12 oz. lump crab meat

1/3 cups green onions, finely minced

6 Tbsp. GF all purpose flour

2 tsp. **Virtuous Living Love** spice

1 tsp **Virtuous Living Hope** spice

1-½ tsp chia seeds, ground

1 clove garlic, minced

1/4 cup mayonnaise

3 Tbsp. water

1-½ Tbsp. fresh lemon juice

1 tsp. dijon mustard

Ghee or coconut oil for cooking

Directions:

In a bowl, mix chia seeds, lemon juice and water together. Allow this mixture to stand about 5 minutes, until thick. Add the rest of your ingredients to the bowl and mix until thoroughly combined. Reserve cooking oil. Scoop crab meat mixture into 1/2 inch thick patties. The cakes should be about 1/4 cup in size. Heat ghee or coconut oil in a large skillet over medium-high heat. Pan fry each cake one or two at a time, until golden brown. Drain excess oil by placing cooked crab cakes on a paper towel. Squeeze half a lemon wedge over the cakes and garnish with fresh parsley and homemade Remoulade sauce. Crab cakes can also be baked on a greased baking sheet.

Remoulade Sauce

1 cup Mayonnaise

2 tsp Dijon mustard

1/12 tsp whole grain mustard

1 tsp white wine vinegar

1 tbsp Extra virgin olive oil

1/4 tsp. Frank's Hot sauce (its GF)

2 tsp capers, drained, minced

1 tbsp parsley, chopped

1 small shallot

Virtuous Living Himalayan Pink Salt and freshly ground black pepper to taste

Classic Oven Roasted Chicken

Ingredients:
1, 3-5lb. organic whole chicken

2-3 organic lemons

3/4 cup organic butter, softened

4 sprigs of organic thyme, and rosemary (2 each)

4 Tbsp. **Virtuous Living Love** spice blend

Salt and pepper (for inside cavity)

Directions:
Preheat oven to 450*

In a small bowl mix softened butter, chopped herbs, and Love. Place your washed, and pat dry chicken on a prep board. Tie the legs together with kitchen twine, and tuck the wings under. Generously salty and pepper the inside cavity of the chicken. Squeeze the juice from your lemons over the chicken and stuff 2-3 halves of lemon and a few sprigs of fresh herbs into the chicken cavity. Now its time to give your chicken a good massage. Massage the buttery-herby-spice mixture onto the chicken. Make sure to get the mixture into all the nooks and crannies, inside the cavity, and under the skin. This is what will flavor the entire bird. After thoroughly covering, place the chicken in a roasting pan breast up. Be sure to carfeully clean your hands, utensils and prep surfaces with an anti-bacterial spray once you finish handling the chicken.

Place the chicken in the oven and roast on 450* for 15 minute. Reduce the heat to 325* and finish cooking for 40 minutes or until your chicken is a deep golden color, and the juices and drippings run clear. Remove from oven and allow to rest for 10-15 minutes before carving. Serve with a side salad, or roasted root vegetables.

Steak Frites

Ingredients:

2, 8 oz. flat iron steaks
1 lb. Yukon gold potatoes
1/4 cup organic coconut oil, divided
1/2 cup or 1 stick, salted butter, room temperature
2 tbsp **Virtuous Living Love** spice blend
1/4 cup fresh parsley, chopped fine
Juice from 1 organic lemon
Cracked black pepper
Virtuous Living Himalayan Pink Salt to taste
2 Tbsp. fresh thyme, plus more

Cut potatoes into small wedges, and place into a large container filled with water. Refrigerate for 1 hour. Place steaks in the refrigerator as well.

Directions:

In a bowl. mix 4 tsp butter, herbs, salt, and black pepper. Mix until smooth. Scoop the mixture out onto plastic wrap and roll it into the shape of a log. Seal the ends, and refrigerate until firm.

Remove potatoes, or frites from refrigerator. Heat a cast iron skillet, or any other oven safe skillet, on medium high for 1 minute. Add 2 tsp. coconut oil and place frites flat in skillet. Drizzle with 1 tsp coconut oil, and sprinkle with fresh herbs. Place in oven a cook for 25-30 minutes. Be sure to check your potatoes, turning them occasionally so they brown evenly on all sides. Remove from oven and transfer to a plate.

Remove steaks from the fridge. Unwrap, and wipe gently with a damp paper towel. Season with "Love", on both sides. Using a cooking towel, gently wipe out all the remaining bits from the cast iron skillet that you made the fries. Place the skillet on the stove on high heat. Add whats left of your coconut oil to the pan, add steaks and 1 tbsp of butter. Reduce heat to medium-high, and flip after the first side has browned, about 1 minute. Gently tilt the pan and baste the steaks using a large spoon with the pan juices while they cook for 2 more minutes on the second side. Turn stove off, and transfer skillet to the oven to cook for 4-5 more minutes for Medium-rare. 6 minutes if you want Medium- Medium well. I recommend Medium for this recipe.

Chicken Enchilada stuffed-Spaghetti Squash

Ingredients:
2 -8oz boneless organic chicken breasts

1 2 1/2 lb. pound spaghetti squash, halved and seeded

3 cups diced tomatoes

1 cup tomato puree

1 Jalapeño pepper

1-2 tsp **Virtuous Living Hope** spice blend

2 tsp Cumin

1 tbsp minced organic garlic

1 tbsp chili powder

2 tsp lemon or lime juice

1-2 cups of chopped kale

1 cup of shredded organic grass fed Jack Cheese

Salt and pepper to taste

Directions:
Preheat oven to 400*. Place squash, face up and already halved, on a baking sheet in the oven to roast 30-40 minutes or until tender. On another greased baking sheet, place seasoned chicken into the same oven. Bake chicken breasts until golden brown and the juices run clear. Remove the chicken from the oven and allow to rest. Keep watching your squash, and remove when tender and slightly golden.

In a sauce pan, make your sauce by adding your diced tomatoes, tomato puree, chopped kale, peppers, herbs and spices and bring to a slow simmer. Add 1/2 cup of water if your sauce seems thick. Season with salt and pepper to taste. Transfer to a bowl, reserving about 2-3 tbsp. for later. Once chicken has cooled, shred it with 2 forks. Transfer to a seperate bowl. Using a different fork, gently scrape the inside of the squash into the bowl with the sauce. Set your empty squash shells to the side for later.

Add your shredded chicken to the sauce mixture and toss, coating well. Transfer the mixture of squash, chicken, kale, and herbs back into the squash shells. Top with leftover sauce and cheese. Place the stuffed squash back in the oven on the middle rack for about 10 minutes, or just until cheese is melted and golden.

Serve with a side salad, and Mexican hot chocolate for dessert.

Dressings

Honey Citrus Vinaigrette

1 small shallot, minced
3 tablespoons of citrus vinegar
Virtuous Living Himalayan Pink Salt, to taste
2 tsp organic, raw honey
fresh cracked black pepper
6 tbsp organic olive oil

Use immediately

Thai Lime Dressing

5 large garlic cloves, minced
2 Serrano or similar green chilies, shredded,
minced 4 teaspoon raw cane sugar
2 tbsp GF Tamari (like soy sauce)
1/4 cup fresh squeezed lime juice
2 tsp black and white sesame seeds, divided
1 cup Organic Olive oil

Use immediately

Balsamic Vinaigrette

3 tbsp balsamic vinegar
1 Tbsp dijon mustard
1 clove garlic
1/2 cup organic olive oil
Virtuous Living Himalayan Pink Salt, to taste
fresh cracked black pepper

Use immediately or refrigerate for up to 4 days

Desserts

Vegan Avocado Chocolate Mousse

4 very ripe avocados
1/2 cup organic putted dates
1/4 cup organic maple syrup
1/2 cup organic unsweetened cocoa powder
1/3 cup coconut milk (full-fat)
1 tsp. organic Vanilla extract
Pinch of **Virtuous Living Himalayan Salt**

Directions:
Combine all ingredients in a food processor on high speed powered blender until smooth. Pour or spoon into individual ramekins and refrigerate for at least 2 hours.

For thicker mousse, simply use less milk. Recipe can be prepared up to 1 day in advance. Garnish with toasted pistachios, fresh berries, or sliced oranges. Serve chilled.

*Avocados go bad quickly so eat immediately, and only store for 1 day.

Vanilla Bean Gelato

Ingredients:
2 1/4 cups whole goat milk (or milk of your choice)
3/4 cup full fat coconut cream
1 vanilla bean, split lengthwise
3/4 cup monkfruit sweetner
1 tsp **Virtuous Living Faith** spice
2 tbsp. Arrowroot powder
1 egg yolk

Directions:
Put 1 1/4 cups of the milk, cream, and vanilla bean into a heavy-bottomed saucepan and heat over medium heat until bubbles appear around the edge of the saucepan and mixture is about to boil. Put remaining 1 cup milk, monkfruit sweetner, and arrowroot powder into a small bowl and stir until well combined. Remove saucepan from heat and stir in arrowroot mixture. Return saucepan to medium-low heat and cook, stirring frequently, until sweetners and Faith dissolve and mixture thickens slightly, 8-10 minutes. Remove saucepan from heat.

Place an egg yolk into a medium bowl and whisk thoroughly. Pour 1 cup of the hot milk mixture into the bowl with the yolk, whisking constantly, then gradually add the yolk mixture back into the hot milk mixture in the saucepan, stirring with a wooden spoon. This process is called tempering, and its important so your egg yolk doesn't cook in the hot liquid and cause it to look like scrambled egg milk! Once you've completed this step, set the mixture aside in a glass bowl to let cool, stirring often. Remove and discard vanilla bean.

Using an ice cream maker, pour the cooled mixture into your machine and follow the directions to finish your gelato.

Grandma Fannie's World Famous Baked Apples

Ingredients:

4 of your favorite apples

2 Tbsp **Virtuous Living Faith** spice

1/2 tsp organic maple syrup

1 pat of butter or ghee to top each apple

1 tsp organic vanilla extract

1 pinch **Virtuous Living Himalayan Pink Salt**

Directions:

Pre-heat oven to 350*.

Wash and core apples and pat dry. Slice the top off of each apple, and set aside. Place apples into a buttered oven-safe baking dish. In a small bowl mix syrup, vanilla and for a delicious twist, add a sprinkle of cardamom. Sprinkle Faith on top of apples. Drizzle with maple mixture and top with organic butter. Bake for 15-20 minutes or until apples are tender.

Remove from heat and baste in juices. Place back in the oven until just golden brown. Remove and allow to cool slightly. Serve with Vanilla bean Gelato.

Strawberries with Balsamic Vinegar

Ingredients:
4 pints (8 cups) fresh, organic strawberries, sliced thick
5 tablespoons balsamic vinegar
2 tablespoons of **Virtuous Living Faith** spice
1/4 teaspoon freshly ground black pepper
2 pints vanilla ice cream, or vanilla bean gelato (see page147) for serving
Freshly grated lemon zest, for serving

Directions:
Thirty minutes to an hour before serving, combine the strawberries, balsamic vinegar, Faith, and pepper in a bowl. Set aside at room temperature.

Place a serving of ice cream in a bowl, and top with a serving of the strawberries and sauce. Garnish with lemon zest.

"Our bodies are our gardens —our wills are our gardeners."

-William Shakespeare

Afterword

My Grandfather was not a big fan of going to the doctor's office. That had to rank as one of his least favorite places to go to. Something would have to be literally falling off before he would go and even then it was still be very reluctantly. My Grandmother, who I called **Ning**, knew this and I remember her healing most of his ailments with food. I remember seeing my Grandmother make food for my Grandfather that she knew would improve his overall mental, physical and emotional state of mind. I remember hearing her say that eating this was good for his liver or good for his heart. Or eating this was good for his kidneys or would stop his headache. I remember her giving him food that she said would help his digestive system or knock out his chest or head cold or pull the toxins out of his system. My Grandfather just went along with whatever the food was as long as it tasted good. I remember literally seeing him come home in a bad mood, eat and then magically be in a good mood. And not just because he was hungry and was no longer hungry after eating, but his actual entire spirit would change. I remember hearing my Grandmother talk about the healing power of food. I didn't know what she was talking about then, I was a little kid, but I remember hearing her saying the words. That's why it was almost eerie to hear my wife Nichole say some of the same things I remember my Grandmother used to say. Stressing the importance of what you put into your body and how detrimental it can and will be if you put the wrong things in. Or that what you eat is directly tied to your emotional, spiritual and physical health and that you can actually heal your body with food or cutting out certain foods. My wife always says that every believer's birthright is optimal health and if Jesus died on the cross for all of our sins, sickness and diseases, optimal health should be obtainable. She also says that Faith, Family, Food and Fun will get you back to health and furthermore, how important it is to understand what specifically will feed your spirit. And just like my Grandfather, I go along with whatever she cooks and have no objections and really don't even ask any questions, my only requirement is that it tastes good. And that hasn't been a problem yet.

I am always amazed to see so many modern women who have absolutely zero interest in cook-ing. Who literally eat fast food and take out and grub hub all the time. I remember hearing one of my teamate's girlfriend in particular say that the only thing she knew how to make were reservations, and she said it so proudly. That entire concept was just so foreign to me because my wife uses food for everything the same was my Grandmother did.

I was always someone who had relatively decent eating habits. I was a professional athlete so there were certain types of foods that just wouldn't be conducive to optimal performance on the court for a professional athlete. However, I have also seen my share of guys who don't take care of their health. On the outside, they may appear to be in tip top shape, or even on top of the world, but if you pull back they layers, they are in emotional, spiritual, and physical turmoil. Many people don't see how these three things are even connected, I sure didn't know. As I said I just ate what my wife gave me as long as it tasted good, but after reading why she prepared food the way she did, I see that everything was for a particular reason.

Something else I picked up from my Grandfather is that I'm not a big fan of going to the doctor. I'll go maybe a little before something is falling off but not too much before. I have been blessed just the way my Grandfather was blessed to have a wife who knows how to cook to heal, balance, relax, nurture, comfort, and support. It's amazing what you can do with the right food. I believe that God gives us the helpmate we need in order to be successful and that's why **Proverbs 18:22** says,

"He who finds a wife finds a good thing and obtains favor from the Lord"

- Etan Thomas
former NBA Veteran and Proud husband

CPSIA information can be obtained
at www.ICGtesting.com
Printed in the USA
LVHW01*1436290118
564432LV00025B/441/P